To Martha —
A dear & precious
creative friend!
Love & Blessings! Tamara
3-17

Tamara Smiley Hamilton

Illustrations by E.J. Hobson

Soul Quake/by Tamara Smiley Hamilton—First Edition

1. Poetry 2. African American women

Editor: Branita Griffin Henson
Designers: Brett Rand Guldemond and Catherine Rawson Guldemond, Rand & Rawson Design
Cover Art/Illustrations: E. J. Hobson
Production Manager: Robert C. Hamilton

10 9 8 7 6 5 4 3 2

Published by NETvision
PO Box 183
Herndon, VA 20172-0183
www.soulquake.com
703-471-5577

ISBN: 0-9778559-0-2

F.J. Hobson

Feel the earth rock… Feel the soul quake…

Dedication

For Robert C. (Tau) Hamilton and Paulette (Gem) Hobson
The greatest thing is love...

For my three sons: Mossi Tau Hamilton, Maso Toussaint Hamilton and Mikhail T. Hamilton
Thank you for loving and protecting me enough to keep me in the gym...

For Edis, Ericka, and Evan Hobson
Follow your dreams.

And for the precious and sacred life of
Gem Marie Hobson (1977-2002)
God kissed your soul and set you free.

For Adrian Dante Victorian (1984-2003)
We sure do miss you.

For Frederick Dwayne Nichols (1953-1997)
We still feel your smile.

For George E. Johnson (1949-1974)
Viet Nam should have been enough. May we study war no more?

Maso Smiley (1920-1967)
I did it, Daddy! Just like you said: "Be somebody to help somebody."

For Katie L .Smith (1887-1986)
My original sistafriend who taught me discipline and patience through the art of crochet.

And for my German families who demonstrated unconditional love in
the days of Kindsbach, Rhineland-Phalz (pop. 3500):
Frau Halvas who taught me to knit socks and introduced me to the opera and Puccini...
Familien Berberich, Familien Scherdel, Familien Schlissner—
you helped me raise beautiful sons.

To The Golden Circle of the Soul Quake Experience: you made the 37 year dream come true.

***

For Christopher Jackson, Sr.
When the drive-by came home, you took the bullet for all of us.
God will pour you out a blessing.

4

Acknowledgements

My sister, Evelyn Jackson, nineteen years my senior, always knew. She saw and encouraged the writer in me from the very beginning. When she read an original birthday card I gave her just last November, she marveled at the words and said it again, "You went into the wrong field. You ought to be a writer!" When our father died when I was fifteen, she trusted me with her credit cards, kept me whole, and sent me off to Scripps College with my head held high, never feeling like I was less than the rich girls with yachts. I am grateful that she can hold this book in her hands and see the results of her unconditional love and faith in me. My brother-in-law, Willie Jackson, Sr., who combed my hair and sent me off to school with pride, I love you.

My 88-year-old mother, Viney B. Smiley, our Ma'Dear, I look into her loving face and see my future. She always said my ship would come in, although it seemed adrift at sea for many years. My brothers, William S. Smiley and Dino Smiley, "The Godfather of Street Ball"—they have always been my best coaches, my port in the storm. For Julie Peppars, Deniese Hayes, Tahirah Asim-Ali, and Odessa Taylor, the friends who knew me when. And for all of my family: Stephanie Smiley, Chaniel Smiley, Desmond Smiley, Charlene Brown Smiley, Samantha Smiley, Christopher and Makeba Jackson, the twins Malcolm and Malik, Christopher Jackson, Jr., Makia Jackson, Marcus Franklin, Willie Jackson, Jr., Williesha Jackson. My mother-in-law, Dorothy Nichols, who keeps me spiritually grounded. For Kenneth Nichols, Doreen Nichols, Leah Nichols, Michael Terry Nichols, Donna Nichols, Malcolm and Michael Nichols, Donnie Nichols, Crissy Nichols, Fred Nichols, Brett Nichols, and Debbie Nichols, John H. Howard, Ernestine Howard, Allison Howard, Jamal Howard, Louise Howard, and George Howard.

And with very special love, my uncle, Sandy Smiley, Mary Smiley, Sheron Smiley Cuffee Johnson, Michael Johnson, Jared Johnson, and the beautiful Holland Johnson.

In deep appreciation: my editor, Branita Griffin Henson, who guided me with the love and patience of the dearest sisterfriend. You will always be in my heart. I am humbled by your kindness. For Sewell B. Johnson who seemed to always be there before I needed his advice. David Morris, Dennis Slaughter, Doc Powell, and Marge Laney, thank you for all you did to help me. And, Catherine and Brett Guldemond, the creative couple of Rand and Rawson, simply awe-inspiring to work with you. And Rachel Frazier of Wondrous Works, who put together the initial draft of Soul Quake in 1997, so I had something to hold in my hands. Evon and Lennell: priceless friends.

For my mentors who gave me guidance when I needed it most: Dr. John F. Leeke, Evelyn Temple, Deloris Edwards Rozier, Vade Bolton, the late Georgia Maryland, Nelson Okino, Eva McLain, and Dr. Debbie Jackson…and all of the Interns. Special thanks to the National Black Staff Network for giving me opportunities to share my creativity.

In gratitude and respect, Nancy Trask, a White woman who in 1968 met a sixteen year old Black girl at the Brotherhood/Any Town Camp on top of the Idyllwild Mountains, and changed my life forever. Perhaps through this publication, we will see each again.

Table of Contents

Feel the Earth Rock... Feel the Soul Quake

God Kissed Your Soul

A Stab Wound to the Heart

Epilogue

"When anger throws a party,
do I go?"
—Georgia Hedrick

E.J. Hobson

Why I Write

Sometimes I wonder what people will say when they read my poetry when I am not around to interpret the mirrors of my soul. It would be interesting and frightening to be that fly on the wall, silently perched on the mantel, antennae alert, listening to my words speaking for me. Maybe some light will be shed for me, too. But, in the meantime, I just write to unleash a pregnant spirit that wants to share so much with so many.

My life has been good, bordering on greatness. I can say this even though when the bills are paid I will not be able to buy a dress on sale or upgrade my underwear. My life has been good and bordering on greatness because my vision is expanded into both the past and future. It makes the present so much easier to conquer.

I have three sons in need of images. I write for many reasons, but now my legacy is theirs. How proud they will be to read a poem in class and say, "My mom wrote that."

I have a husband who really likes me while loving me a whole lot. My stories of survival and growth are dedicated to him. He was that missing piece that rounded my fullness. It is wonderful to have a live-in coach, a cheerleader who believes in my dreams as much as I do.

I write because I have a gift with words and feel the need to chronicle the times. In these times of violence and beauty, of youth feared by many, and music that promotes sex in a time of AIDS, there has to be a vision that helps us to understand these perilous periods of passing through generations.

I write because stories, lyrics, and rhythms jump in my head and won't let me rest until they are given life on paper. It's a sharing thing, a way to give a gift that can raise hopes, pull smiles out of sorrows, and make someone somewhere say, "Ah."

Who will speak the truth to the people if not us?

Gather round all the children
and listen to me
there's a world outside
I want you to see...

The Blessing in the Beauty

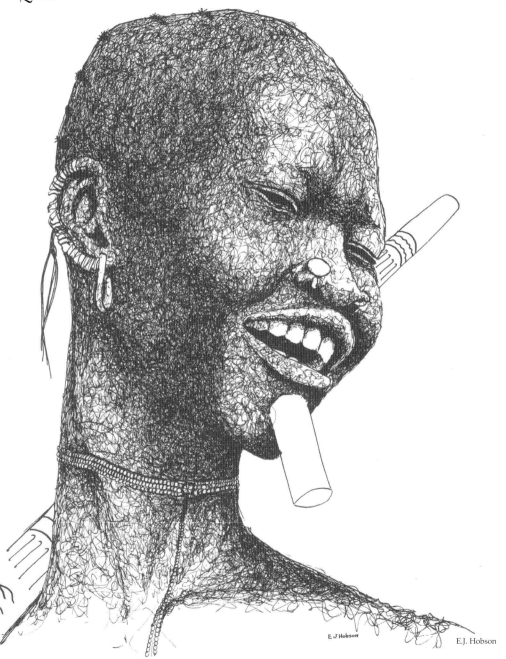

E.J. Hobson

My Joy

(For Robert C. Hamilton)

When you look into my face
and see a glow,
it's because of the
love I know:
cool as
a summer's breeze—
gentle tonic
putting fears at ease.

The blessing in the beauty
of the spirit dance:
those steps I glide through
to get to you.

Love

Love makes you do crazy stuff:

stuff you can only tell a friend
a good friend
at that.

Love makes you stupid.

But love makes you real.

Happy in Love

Our children full of grace

Smiles circling their face

If we could love as they do

All of our dreams would come true

Into Our World: A Son

(for Christopher Jackson, Jr.)

Into our world: a son
      a spitting image
      a copy originally you

Into our world: a son
      spirit tough
      nerves strong as steel

Into our world: a son
      to hold and cherish
      a fiery soul—too cool

Into our world: a son
      life's joy spreading
      the essence of family

Into our world: a son
      a boy too soon a man
      our future redeemed

Into our world: a son
      strong warrior-manchild
      hearing the battle cry

Into our world: a son
      let us be thankful
      in grace and joy

Into our world: a son
      into our world: a boy.

And a Child Shall Lead the Way

(for Christopher Jackson, Sr.)

You grew up right
in front of our eyes
like a tree—your branches strong:
to hold a son, a future
coming boldly into now

You grew up right
here in our hearts
a special boy
your smile unlocking souls from cobwebs
keeping hope alive

You grew up right
to show us the way:
your courage as eyes for us all
moving into a world
tumbling much too fast.

E.J. Hobson

19

Haiku

No. 1

I sprinkle my love out
to you like sugar
sweetness for your day.

No. 2

Every town has a special sound
a bell tolling…
a siren careening

No. 3

The tulips stayed in
the world's too cold
beauty needs sunlove

No. 4

Friends are sparkling rubies
too priceless to flaunt
too precious to neglect

Upswing

Today was poetic—
moving in the syncopated rhythms
of Hughesian description.
Flowers, tired of peeping
in anticipation of spring,
asserting themselves quite boldly,
stood at attention like top heavy sisters
so very proud of their pulchritude.

It was nice:
a mellow high…
contact in the air
breezing through all the right parts
of places that like
to be tingled (in my body).

Today was a musical:
a song in a shuffle along style
recalling fragrant memories
of springs ago.
Movement was the call of the day;
no time for idleness;
no room for inertia. Energy—
the essence of living.

Today was a musical poem:
a song snapping to the upswing of life.

Celebration!

My children:

they are carnival rides
cotton candy
sweet and dandy.

They set my soul free
singing loud with glee

My children:
so wonderful to me.

They make me glad to be
just me:
a woman whole
strong and bold
carefree in my love.
No strings attached;
I can just relax

My children:

a symphony
playing just for me
harmonious melody—ahhh…
A love supreme
majestic soul force

My children loving me

freeing me
nurturing me—
A life potion
medicine for immortality.

I love on!

Tau at 45

"Let him kiss me with the kisses of his mouth: for thy love is better wine."
Song of Solomon 1:2

At twenty nine when I met you,
You were strong, mellow, and had a
different presence about you: not too cool
not too aggressive—just bold and secure
in yourself and our culture.

I still remember the note
posted on your wall:
"The work habit, the study habit…" the rest
I guess I did forget

But it stuck with me
like you continue to do
through PMS, the depths of depression,
my own fear of my immortality…

You helped me become my real self
to find strength in my convictions
I will always cherish you for that
for who are we, if not ourselves?

As I look at you at 45,
I see a man who has stood steadfast
in principles no matter who said:
"What?!..You must be jiving!"

Sometimes the voice was mine.

But you are still my Tau:
striving towards excellence,
keeping the family strong
always being our sheltering tree
giving us roots that sink deep
growing into generations

As I love you at 45
I still bend low on my knees

and say, "Thank you, God, for blessing me."
It is always so humble and whispered
only into the side of our bed,
but it is the least I can say
for having your shoulder anchored to mine.
Always strong when I am weak:
positive when negativity swallows me.

All birthdays are different
because we change—every seven years, they say.

This one comes with few presents to hold
to wear, to touch and admire, to return for
the better fit.
This one comes with a sizzling love,
a happy heart, a pulsating heart
throbbing always for you.

At 45, we still beat to the same rhythm.

Thank you for enriching my soul
soothing my pain
making me into a woman whole
reaching for new ways to say
through your touch
your squeeze
your sweat melting into mine
that you love me
that you need me
that we will walk a forever path
bearing the thorns
smelling the roses
and always as one body, one soul:
one spirit force.

Happy Birthday, Tau!

"Hear, ye children, the instruction of a father, and attend to understanding…
Wisdom is the principal thing; therefore get wisdom: and with all thy getting get understanding."
Proverbs, 4:1,7

Renewal

The next time

I see love

there won't be

a next time

to turn round

or back

for love

that time's

gon' be mine.

Courtship

Velvet voices slither

through songs singing from the stereo

casting a comfort through the room.

Minds sit still on the couch

moving closer to the spirit.

Eyes, slightly open in a dreamy state,

blinking only to the beat of the bass

far in the background.

In the forefront of the rhythm,

two heads turn a smile into a feeling

as reverberations from the hearts

cause spiritual sensations

to dance between the bodies.

Solo

Fumbling hands drop soapy water
against the shower stall.
I inhale before stepping out.
My nerves won't calm.
The steam can't clear the
mirrored reflection of a face
so strange to gaze upon
in likeness of me.

Dry wrinkled fingers hold tweezers
tight like a vice to pluck
the weight from above my eyes.
I cough clearing phlegm
to be clean for you.

Reggae music dances outside
the bathroom door. Candle smoke
embraces incense like a couple
on a bedroom floor. My best
potion sprays behind erogenous
zones for your searching tongue

to take what it owns. I smile
to make friends with the looking glass.
(It worries me.)

Naked and wired hot
sparking in my movements,
I exit slowly
so slowly that I feel
like crawling on all fours
(If I knew it would move you)
I wallow out in a snake slither
encased in a pea green body stocking.

The clock tells two a.m.
to push on
to push on
to bed alone
with only my bath foam freshness
to caress goodnight.

Plea

Take both my hands

and spread them wide

from the fingers. Feel

the blood rush to the tips

with the throbbing beat of

excited pulsations. Lift

them most graciously to your lips.

Suck my spirit as it squirts

throughout your soul

as it squirts throughout your soul.

A Wedding Song
For Marge and Jim

Cradle us in warm wishes
And words of togetherness
This is a love thing
A forever thing
A love supreme

Bless us in joy
Beyond the morning
Inside the cold of winter
And the soothing spring

This is a love thing
A forever thing
A love supreme

Two souls blending at the heart
Love is all there is
A comfort, support
The light at the tunnel's end

This is a love thing
Joined by commitment
Blessed by friends and family

Starting New: Becoming Whole

Life brings in a new beginning
like the first snow of winter
or the cool of a baby's breath.
In the arms of God
I cradle my fears
let go of my pain
because I have the long
strong love of family.

Men to help me grow stronger:
Robert
Tau
Maso
Mikhail
my heroes all different… all strong and loving me.

Life brings in a new beginning
incipit vita nova: to begin a new life
free of trouble
free of stress
full of the sunshine of spring
and the sweet smell of
Stargazer lilies.

Sweet dreams wait for me
bringing morning filled with freshness
a dewdrop on the maple leaves
cleansing rain for the soul
life brings a sweet start
a new start of health and happiness
a season of joy and giving
letting all of my creativity flow
and flow
and flow
straight to the heart of my family—
loving men who love me
protect me and say:
"You're okay."

For Tau

A good man is you
massaging fragile wings,
a shade tree in the August sun

Dilemmas in a Nightmare at High Noon

E.J. Hobson

Poetry Painting

If I could write passionate poetry
the kind that stirs deep behind the navel
I would capture the beauty of the skies
and the blue deep as the heavens

I would gather the sound of ocean waves
and the spirit of dolphins swimming
the beauty of whales diving in the dawn
If I could write passionate poetry…

I would make words sing in the Sierras
against the backdrop of Lake Tahoe
songs sparkling in the soul
making birds soar into its beauty

If I could write passionate poetry
my words would waltz the night away
dancing on silk chords of joy
all the children laughing in love

If I could write passionate poetry
weapons would drop into the deep well
bulldozed over in our collective pain
we won't study war—
on each other—
no more
If only I could...

E.J. Hobson

Looking Back

Today I'm looking back
Don't want my dreams to crack
to crinkle jaggedly into ash:
today, I'm looking back

Dilemma Dealing

(For Warlene Gary)

Decisions—
      got to make them
              before they break me
                    into a thousand pieces
                           of dreams
deferred

Dilemmas in a nightmare
      at high noon.

Decisions—
      got to make them
      the hard kind that shatters
      lives to save my own
                 at forty something

Where is the gold
the honey pot at the
rainbow's end?

Did I sleep through it

                or

                        Did it pass me by?

Signals—
      Signs—
              Read all about it!:
"Woman leaves home to find space."

Dilemma dealing
      decisions: the hard ones
                      to save my life.

Texas Blues Song

I've got a sweet heart in Texas
but I can't call
I've got me a sweet heart in Texas
but I can't call

Cause he's got a wicked wife
who lives to bring me strife
I say he's got a wicked wife
who lives to bring me strife.

One day I'm gonna get a big long kitchen knife
say one day I'm gonna get a big long kitchen knife
One day I'm gonna get that knife
and take her very life.

But I can't do that right now
cause he still loves her so
I say I can't do that right now
cause he still loves her so.

He loves that mean ol' woman
just as much as he loves me
I know he loves that mean ol' woman
much as he loves me.

So for now that's just the way it's got to be
It's just the way it's got to be

Him loving her as much as he love me
Him giving her good loving jes like he do me.

I didn't make this world
and it ain't even fair
That's why me and that woman
done learned to share.

We share all his pain and his ornery ways.
We share all his pain and his mean ol' ways
but when it's my turn for loving,
all I can do is give praise!

I got me a sweet heart in Texas,
but I can't even call
I got me a sweet man in Texas
that I can't even call.

That's why I just drink this gin
and bang my head against this rugged wall.

Jes drink this ol' gin
and bang my head against this rugged wall
against this rugged wall.

Silence

silence sounds
like sugar swept
from the table

silence feels
like a kiss blown
across the field

silence comforts
like the cool hand
on a feverish stomach

silence hugs
like the deep
velvet of night

silence listens
while we talk to God

E.J. Hobson

A Love Song to Someone
Who Could Have Been Loved

Today:
You would be talking
and running all over me
Getting into my lotions and powders
spilling his cologne.

Just think:

How beautiful you would have been
only two feet from the ground
and still growing faster.
You would have had lots of friends
to come to your parties.
And I would have fixed cakes
with Pillsbury mix, Duncan Hines frosting
with a football in the middle.
You'd have loved it to death!
I would have let you eat until your very brown
and very bright eyes bulged out
like the pink little mouse I would have given you
which he gave me
at Disneyland
so long ago
so very long ago.
I was saving it for you.

I wonder if your eyes would have been mine
or his
would your smile have been too broad
like mine
and would you have shook all over
especially at the shoulders
like he does
when you laughed.
I wonder.

It's kind of hard to tell now
it's been so long.
I used to be able to see you
to hold you
to stop the tears.
But now I can't even remember your tears
mine are always in the way.

I really wonder now:
after things have passed,
I really wonder…
Was it worth the lost?
Did I really gain by destroying you—
or was it me?
I've asked my soul,
but it isn't there.

Resolution

Wouldn't miss him
Wouldn't miss him
Wouldn't miss him not one bit
Said I wouldn't miss him
Wouldn't miss miss
But
Didn't know it'd be like this
Like this, like this, like this
Didn't know it was gon be like this

Way in the night
I feel his hand
Creeping round my shoulders
Up and down around my shoulders
Way in the night
Just fore the crack o' day
Could hum his tune
As he blew pine needles my way
Dartin' in and out my skin
Acidic jabs going in and in and in
Could hum his tune
As it blew through to my way
All the way in my way

My God! Wish I'd knowed it'd be
this bad, that I'd feel so sad
Just cause he left
Just cause he left like the wind
Just cause he came and left
Like the pinch of the March wind…
And me?

I was just a leaf
A raw, itching leaf
Looking for a place to fall
Looking over earth's dusty blanket
For an orgasmic place to fall
To drift from here to there
To drift from here to there

Cause I knew this time
Was the last time to fall real hard
Feet first

Head last
Don't want no time to think
About the one thing I'm doing best
About this thing I'm doing

Axim

Axim is like a poem:
it moves and dances
to the rhythms of the heart.

Axim is like a song:
it flows throughout my soul,
an ebbing tide at twilight.

At dusk
as the sun eases down
dipping into the sea
fisherman float
on a billowed blanket of peace.

Axim: relaxed mood
easy quiet at harmattan.

The Mission

Go through a change—
a new head trip
to cope with disappointments
that have no right to be.
Go towards a better definition of life
to ease the rough spots on the road to serenity.

Serenity: a journey ventured by many
but completed only by those determined to be happy;
determined to be at peace
with the mind and the soul…
With life's ups and downs.
Peace will not find me.
I will have to seek it out
In all things that I do.

Silence (Encore)

We sit in this room
Silence heavy like gloom
Before a storm
In control
We speak in tones
Polite, even—leaving
Passion perched in the
Molding—looking down on us
Silence barks
It heaves a heavy sigh
Each of us looking down
Around and sideways out
Seeking a space
To place
Feelings undiscovered
"An unexamined life
Is not worth living."
Laughter soothes
Souls in question
Do I dare?
Should I disclose?
Silence protects me
From all alarm
Leaning into it
Braces my feelings
Giving me an anchor
Got to hold down
A curtain rising
Letting the whole me
Peek out and stare
At a world no
Longer there
I have become free
Once I looked into me.

Journey to Inner Space

Monday. Day three of the journey to Inner Space—
A place where I have not gone before.
Deeper than the Pacific Ocean.
More unsettling than high tide
By the light of the moon.
Sun setting on disillusion.
Awakening to a day in a life
With the promise of
Connections
Integration
Congruence
And Growth.
Day three.
A mark in time.
One small step for me
One giant step for growth.
Rolling back feelings of
Frustration and confusion.
Why does this happen to me?
My intent was…
I meant to say…
I tried to do…
Oh! The places we know
And grow with a small toe
Dipped into feelings.
Deep water on shallow ground.
Hear my cry, Oh Lord.
I want just to be
Me—all of me in
Whole cloth. Seamed
By stitches of love,
Compassion, and
Justice for all.

Feel the Earth Rock...
Feel the Soul Quake

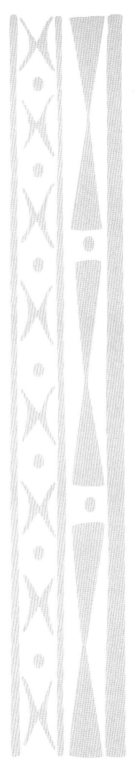

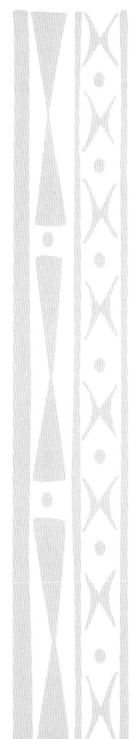

E.J. Hobson

All Voices to the Center

Come to the center
Stay awhile
The ancestors greet you
holding blessings in wrinkled hands
to keep you warm
in the blizzard of life

Come to the center
Stay awhile
You are safe here
The coyotes are asleep
The sniper is on vacation

Come to the center
Stay awhile
Weapons of war
Rust in the acid rain
Let us talk
about community; love is real.

Come to the circle
Rest your heart
and your feet
Smile:
Good times bounce on the rainbow
The ancestors greet you

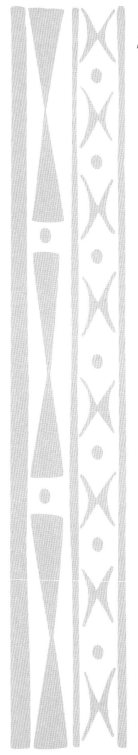

What's IT Like?

It's like having lost children, yet always looking
up to see their faces

It's like a death in the family—everyday

It's like there is always something there to remind you…

It's like seeing friendly faces in your dreams

It's like missing certain kinds of comfort,
a special kind of warmth

It's like knowing the freshness of rain…
and never forgetting the dryness of the drought

It's like starting almost all over again

It's like now you wish you'd gotten around
to it

It's like not truly knowing how the village felt
when a griot died.

It's like losing a library

but living on the Word
The Word.
Words of wisdom,
contradictions, and despair.

E.J. Hobson

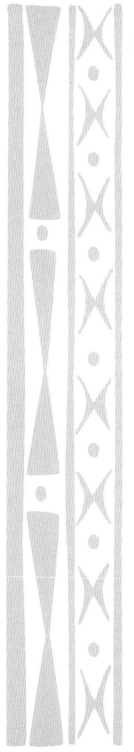

The Long Walk Home

With a rock steady ready rhythm
she moves down dusty highways
crushing the salt of the earth:
the rich red clay—
the promise of a future
between toes calloused by the roads of striving without:
the freedom (oh how good it must feel!)
the man (in the mines three hundred miles away…away…away)

the peace (is it over yonder?)

But…

the love of the baby at her breast is there
the hope for the child becoming full inside her is there
the comfort of the elders around her…
the spirit of the youth ahead of her…
the troubles all around her…
all moving her slide into a stride of strength…

Towards—

the peace: she can feel it
has not had it
but knows it
and loves it
and wants it oh so badly.

As she glides down dusty highways a
tune still parts her chapped lips;
a clap still beats from her soul:
the lilies of the field are still growing
the sparrow in the wind is still eating
and the sun still sets in a kaleidoscope of colors…

As she walks down dusty highways
the plain winds pushing her forward
the baby at her breast sleeping with a smile
she sees the freedom on the sunrise horizon

and hums a prayer for the world.

A Protection Poem for Holland Johnson

Where and when you enter: grace.
standing on the shoulders of ancestors:
a place for you paid for by blood,
sweat, and the tears of struggle.
Where and when you enter: pause
Moments of silence in the space
sacred in honor of fallen soldiers—
men and women of vision
children of hope
peace in a barren land.

When and where you enter: smile.
Storms clearing rainbows,
families across the nation
joining hands to protect you,
to support you,
to cheer you on

Where and when you enter,
many women before you,
proud of you: Holly,
our blessed future,
our promise of a new day.

When and where you enter,
millions drowned
thousands mourned
bodies dangled like strange fruit.

On the shoulders of ancestors,
by the grace of God,
you enter a proud woman
with family at your back—
always lean on our
everlasting arms.

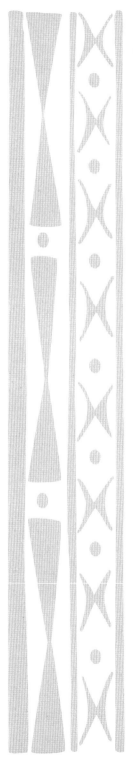

Standing On the Edge of Summer

(On the Occasion of the Marriage of Mary Canty and Herbert Merrill)

As we stand on the edge of Summer:
moonbeams on the left
rainbows on the right—
witnesses gathered on southern soil
close to our ancestors
nodding "Amen"

Feel the soul quake
feel the earth rock
feel the energy bouncing:
electric love
a new family begins;
living as two ends
yielding to the power of one.

"Oh, Mary don't you weep…"

A Love Supreme…

On this day the good race has been run
a new day has begun
when a man loves a woman…
a forever friend
a whisper in the dark
a candle in the night
hands rest on your shoulder
forever cradling your fears
softening your tears
bringing smiles just because…

"A good man is so very hard to find…"

On this day: we say
"Skies of blue, clouds of joy
Oh! What a wonderful world…"
A man and a woman

the sister, the brother, the son and the daughter
of generations that paved the path
of unconditional love:
even when we could not marry
those dark days ago.

We gather on southern soil on the edge of Summer:
A community of witnesses
a warming time
a soothing time:

to feel, to hear, to exhale
to give one united:

Heart beat
Heart beat
Heart beat

Life living in love
on the edge of Summer

In this quiet space
we affirm that for every time there
is a season and a reason
under heaven—

For after all,
the greatest thing is love.

On the edge of Summer
On the edge of Summer
On the edge of Summer

Incipit vita nova:
a new beginning.

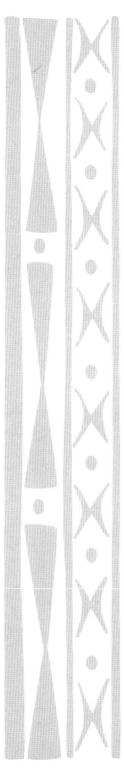

Meditation

We walk by the sea
and be close,
calm as the star
floating in the sky,
as near as waves
kissing the night
on the deep horizon.

Meditation 2

I love to watch the
waters off African shores
under the iridescent light
of a quarter moon
so much silence heard
in so much space in time
as I watch the waters
off African shores
guided by nature's light.

Influencing Effectively: A Delicate Art

Timing, flexibility, patience, awe:
Going with the flow
To get in the know

Trusting the process
Moving in…graciously
Moving together…in harmony
Moving out…on a path
Moving apart…to a future

Pacing, rhythm, energy, synergy
Going with the flow
To get in the know

Influencing effectively:
A delicate art

Kid Power

Children are
the future hope—
let's keep them safe
away from dope
Give them room to grow
the will to live
the need to
know

God Kissed Your Soul

E.J. Hobson

A Song for Gem Marie

Gem-Gem Gem-Gem Gem-Gem Marie
God kissed your soul
And set you free

Gem-Gem Gem-Gem Gem-Gem Marie
Your love lives on
Eternally

Gem-Gem Gem-Gem Gem-Gem Marie
God kissed your soul
And set you free

Gem-Gem Gem-Gem Gem-Gem Marie
You now walk in love
With the Angels above

Flashing that smile
That warms the heart
From our embrace
You'll never depart

Gem-Gem Gem-Gem Gem-Gem Marie
God kissed your soul
And set you free

When the rain pours down
And the sun shines bright
God reminds us
That you are all right

Gem-Gem Gem-Gem Gem-Gem Marie
Our precious love
You'll always be

Gem-Gem Gem-Gem Gem-Gem Marie
God kissed your soul
And set you free

Jump Rope Song for the 90s

When I grow up and count to one
My work will have just begun

When I grow up and count to two
I will know just what to do

When I grow up and count to three
I'll know how things ought to be

When I grow up and count to four
I want gangs to exist no more

When I grow up and count to five
I must keep our hope alive

When I grow up and count to six
I'll hit the bad guy with a brick

When I grow up and count to seven
I'll turn my eyes and look to heaven

When I grow up and count to eight
I'll rest my soul at the pearly gate

When I grow up and count to nine
I'll eat peach cobbler so divine

When I grow up and count to ten
Gangs can't hurt our Black men.

A Sister's Party

"Let the circle be unbroken…"
          there is a legacy here
          of sisters gathering
          to share soul quakes
          to hold dreams of togetherness
close to the heart

"Let the circle be unbroken…"
          the queens of Africa are smiling
          on us—a tradition carried on:
          sisters sharing/listening to hearts
          heavy thumps, songs and
sorrows
          gather together in our names

The sisters gathered
to share
to carry a legacy:
sisters of soul
daughters of Africa
new queens of the Nile

Let the circle be unbroken
Let the circle be unbroken

We make the ancestors proud.

When the Brothers Gather

(for Chris and his Fremont friends)

When the brother gather—great joy!

Laughter bounces like new basketballs
on the open court

Real feelings are welcomed here

Good times come back to sit at the edge of the bed
on the chair
to lean against the wall
Times packed full with
the magic moments of high school

Sides ache, tears stream out
the corners of the eyes
This time to signal the love
Remembered, refreshed from years ago—
the magic moments of high school

But don't mention Venice Beach
the old homeless man...
the stab of laughter suffocates
the story
Laughter keeps bouncing like
new basketballs
on the open court

When the brothers gather, there is strength
Each healing the other.

Friendship is like that:
when the brothers gather.

Odessa's Poem at 44

And then there are those friends who cover your soul like a warm quilt
the kind that blankets you in love on the coldest of days
...on the stormiest of nights

There are those friends that seem to have been with you forever
regardless of the weather in the world
or the blizzard of the circumstances

There are those friends who comfort you in memories
of times that escape the crevices of your mind
but bring old smiles of celebrations

There are those friends who tell you like it is
not the way you want it to be
but the way you need to feel it in the moment

There is only one friend, though,
who has always been there
who has always shared the South Central memories:

Twenty Third Street
Miss Pullum's Cafe
Twentieth Street Elementary School
Forty Ninth Street School
The Telephone Company
The garment district
Paris twice in a weekend
and Cal State LA
Loma Linda
Alprentice and Jason
Tennessee Ratliff: *angels do live on earth*

There are friends who hear your soul in the middle of the night
who feel the power of your dreams and your love of life.
There are friends who can hold your hand across the waters
and there is me: your forever friend: your candle in the dark.

Rejoice

Bad times passing:
a fresh breath from inhaling gasoline

that's how it feels
a weight lifted off the shoulders

Boulders crashing out to sea
bad times passing on

A sour taste on the tongue
cleansed by spearmint hope

Fresh feelings flowing
when bad times pass on

Open up the champagne
fire up the grill
Let the children run and play
adults can cut a rug

Bad times passing: good riddance
Be gone!

Old Friends: For Arlene and Kristie

Old friends: fine wine
A soothing tonic when the lights are low
and crickets sing in the desert wind

Old friends: a comforting soul
like a warm wind in autumn
a fire burning in the winter's cold

Old friends: a hug and a handshake
a poem flowing melodiously
a song singing the good news

Old friends: stability and sureness
a phone call bringing memories closer
to my heart and dreams

Cherish the old friends
they stay with you like a light
on a highway dark and gloomy

Honor the friendship
trust the connection
of old friends: the dearest love

Sistercestors

Energy that suspends me
came straight from you: descendant
of Yaa Asantewa,
the Ghanaian military strategist.
I need you now
more than yesterday.
In this moment I need
to feel your presence—to know
I am the tree that's planted
by the water.
I can't move
away from my direction.
I am on future forward.

Sistercestors:
Rosa, Zora, Nella, Sojourner, Harriet,
Evelyn, Viney, Dorothy, Louise, Katie,
S. Pearl, Beah, Frances,
I call your names now:
To help me stand steady
Rock steady—
A tree that shall not be moved!
"Say it loud: I'm Black and I'm proud!"

Journey to Fulfillment

(for Adair)

The road has rounded: eased into
a soft trail with honeysuckles in the midst.
Potholes are filled where there used to be rain
an outpouring of family songs at high noon.

My ears ring in the silence of mind-peace
the melody is new; the spirit is whole:
Torn souls rejoice to the healing rhythms.

The road has rounded: no peaks, no valleys—
just a flute song in the winter wind
Carrying vibrations of the promised times
the times blending into all tomorrows:

Torn souls rejoice in the healing rhythms
just kick back, lay low
In the healing rhythms of life on high.

Friendship Lament

Once…
I had so many friends
I talked to them through
my answering service

On the waterbed
staring in space
writing a poem

I listened
"Hey girl, call me…"
I'll get back…later

So many friends
I didn't even need to talk to them

"How about dinner at the Red Onion?
Call me…okay? Bye!"

I'll get back…tomorrow

Once,
I had so many friends

I just let them drift
around me
like orbiting satellites
never appreciating their brilliance
the color splashes brought into my life

Now…
Away from friends
Alone in Europe
Too expensive to call
Too far to visit
Too lonely to write

I long for the time I lost
I long for the conversation

Tomorrow…
Tomorrow…

Never put off a friend for today
that can be gone tomorrow

Planet Party

I'm going to invite you to a party
on Saturn, not at Pizza Hut.

My friends are special: worthy of the heavens!

We need the space to party right
after all, it's to celebrate our friendship

the galaxy is ready
the stars are our headlights

they shoot a path straight to the universe

on Saturn we will feast
drink the merry wine
and sing praises for the peace
we share in our love for each other

Won't you come to my party on Saturn?
We'll ring the roses
and *skip-to-my-Lou*

Come on to Saturn...
I'm waiting for you!

Barcelona '92

They ran with the wind
in Barcelona
poetry in Black motion
a soul beat

Legs stretching to gold
arms pumping silver
bronze gazelles bringing us joy,
a soul beat.

They moved like life on high:
years of practice and pain
melting into golden images,
setting in Spain

Carl, Gwen, Gail, Evelyn
your names sit in our hearts
…Flo Jo…
like family members making us proud.
You did too well, so wonderfully

Poetry in black motion
a soul beat
for the children
to dance and dream.

Blacklight

Shining through
into the beam of spirits
dancing in shadows and moonlight
arms stretching to heaven to drink from
the cloud burst of blue tears;
streaming into silver bands of wisdom.

Laughter storming the skies
bringing quaking souls
to rest:
to breathe,
to wallow,
in the midst of the morning dew:
shining through you to
the children of the future.

Souls shimmy shake to the victory march;
the blood soaked cotton gag
expelled.
Trumpets scream the good news: blacklight
shining in the noon day sun
casting shadows of gold in the meadows
on the hills
over the mountainside

...absorbing all images in likeness of me:
the mother, the father, the child unborn and free
beaming spirit force and making us whole
stretching souls to grow in great glory.

Tambourines sound
the great glory:
take the baton, salute the pride—
wrestle the record right

through the call to bless
the blood of the people,
the fruit of the forest:
the youth wanting peace
in images that heal
the swollen sores of life
with no light to mark the way of the warrior.

...keep shining on
Making us glad to be:
a beacon of blacklight...
shining through
shining through,
shining on.
Weaving sense in a nonsense world....

Transition

(For Sheila Simmons and the Celebration of Ike Tribble's Life)

The hero has a lady
Her eyes focused above
To catch a glimpse
Of her true love…

Under the Jamaican sun
Two hearts joined as one
The hero has a lady:
A precious melody.

The hero has a lady.

Her heart heaves with sorrow,
But joy does come tomorrow.

Sacred Words of Friendship
In honor of Georgia Maryland

("The flowers appear on the earth," ...Song of Solomon, 2:12)

Today is profound;
a thunder clap!

Snap!

A bolt of energy: The Lord is my Shepherd

On this lightening bolt kind of day…
Georgia Maryland has gone away

Purple rain soaks our soul
Forever Georgia's story must be told

Mentor, mother, Bingo Queen
She gave us space to sail a dream

We are better than we are;
She polished us to be a star.

We don't buy our bread
Where we get our meat

Because of Georgia—
Our jobs we'll keep.

Purple are the flowers of your soul…

"Until the daybreak, and the shadows flee away, I will get me to the mountain of myrrh,
and the hill of frankincense
…Song of Solomon, 4:6

*Inspired by the collective energy of the graduates of the National Education Association's
Affirmative Action UniServ Intern Program for Women and Minorities.
The UniServ Pre-Employment Development Program
And the National Black Staff Network.*

A Tribute to the Power of Memory

(For John O. Stocks)

When it's all said and done
It's the little things in life…
The stroll through familiar streets
The diversity of neighborhoods:
the parishes
Music flowing, people laughing, cars passing
On Bourbon Street, to name one…

It's the fun times with friends and family
The dinners, the picnics, the parties
The good times shared late into the evening
Dancing and dancing and dancing
And always finding your way *home*
All over again.

It's the sounds of the city
The smell in the air
The energy bouncing off the French Quarter.
It's the canals, the casinos, the convention goers
The music festivals—

The schools building knowledge:
Xavier, Dillard, LSU, Tulane… the Bayou Classic

It's the smile and passion of
Of Louis Armstrong:
"I say to myself: what a wonderful world…"
Even now in despair and confusion
Chaos and tragedy…

It's a Mardi Gras memory
The splendor and fascination of
The balls and ball gowns
The beads, the gumbo, the candy—
drums drawing you home…
The cadence of the speech
Always welcoming you *home.*

It's the quiet time with memories,
The blessings of the experiences;
The culture of the Big Easy: its soul
will never be washed away.

August 31, 2005

Evon and Zeke

True friends come to you
Without asking
Bringing Psalms 31
And Romans 8

True friends give you shelter
Others can't see
But you feel
Deep inside your soul

True friends speak
Without words
Full of meaning
Support unbridled

True friends bring joy
Without even being there
Like the smile of God
Blowing in the wind

True friends have large
Hearts
Strong shoulders
And funny tales
That take your pain away

True friends check on you
To see how you are doing
Even when you are asleep
Thanking God for them

True friends are you:
Evon and Zeke
Angels on earth
Doing God's work

At Retirement

(For Lynn Ohman)

It's the little things we treasure:
The morning dew at sunrise
The glow of the sun setting in summer
The soft wonder of a baby's breath
The love of friends and family

It's the little things we need:
Strong friendships solid as a rock
Deep relationships that bend
Kindness and forgiveness
Dancing to the old songs

It's the little things we need:
Time to reflect on blessings
Hugs from our children
The love of a good man
The unconditional love of real friends

It's the little things we adore:
Friendship over three decades
Laughter that is timeless
Kindness that is endless
Loyalty that is priceless

And time to breathe.

Praise Song Sunday

(For Rev. Norman A. Tate, Pastor
Heritage Fellowship United Church of Christ)

It is harvest time:
time to kiss rain storms goodbye
and see a bluer sky.
Praise Song Sunday is here.

Time to join hearts
and let souls gather in thanksgiving,
testifying for the gifts.
Praise Song Sunday is here.

No flowers without rain.
No celebration
without pain.
Praise Song Sunday is here.

You have given us your best.
You have stood the test,
being there for all of us:
staying strong under stress

The rainbow is here.
It's time for good cheer.
God's blessing pouring out on this
Praise Song Sunday.

A Stab Wound to the Heart

When the Drive-by Came Home:
A Journal Poem Restructuring Pain
(An Epic of a South Central Family)

When the drive-by came home

vision glowed casting rainbows

on the cloud
the multitude
mass:
the people who love you

Aura sweet eroding
in a pop-pop-pop-pop-pop-

          pop-pop-

                  pop...
              snap of the neck
            crack to the head
        worse than any drug

When the drive-by came home
       twilight zone in the dusk
       pain deep as Bosnia

                in the bowel
                  the center:
          the people who love you

Soul so sweet
       the children grow great
       when learning from you:
               "Be strong when it hurts."

               "Help one another."
                  "It's cool"

Making them whole
at least in that moment
of your attentive glow.

When the drive-by came home
               a stab wound to the heart
               straight
hard
out the back
the word "sad": defined too big for just one family
to feel
aching: earthquake shattered
a constant tremble deep down

When the drive-by came home:

"The Lord is my shepherd:
I shall not want. He maketh me to lie down in green pastures: He leadeth me
beside the still waters. He restoreth my soul: He leadeth in the paths of right-
eousness for his name's sake. Yea though I walk through the valley of the sha-
dow of death I shall fear no evil for thou art with me. Thy rod and thy staff they
comfort me. Thou preparest a table before me in the presence of mine enemies:
Thou anointed my head with oil: my cup runneth over. Surely goodness and
mercy shall follow me all the days of my life and I will live in the house of the
Lord forever." Amen

Two shooters aiming on one
torching spirits of family
and friends
Black kids dreaming stronger dreams:
the boogey-man lives next door
walks to the liquor store
hears the same music we do

Latino kids learning English
faster to talk on the
same plain—as one
with a teacher/coach
creative wisdom
of the game

whatever the sport
When the drive-by came home

spirit warning, maternal gut
some say wisdom
the third eye
labor of love
sight so deep
it still sinks into the future
reverberating into now

When the drive-by came home

        "They're shooting my baby" thundered
in a boom to heaven
the planets
someplace loaded with miracles
"I shall fear no evil..."
Out pouring pain in heaving sobs
the street hugged itself
as one

                                                        not again
                                                           again
                                                           again

                    the gray car gone
                        raping us all

When the drive-by came home

I will paint rainbows for you in hues everlasting:
                    the subtlety of beauty
                    All useful if in place
             colors joining into somewhere else
               ever changing into stronger
                     than what was

Code Blue

We need a code blue
our own signal
for the scoundrels on the loose:

The drive-by cowards
too chicken to fight like
real men used to

So what? A cut, a broken jaw…
A joint out of whack
here and there

"He'll live,"

Everybody knew
When they fought like real men
used to do.

Get down dirty:
Wallow on the ground
Might even pick up a stick
If losing was in sight or coming due
You just get shook up a bit
When they fought like real men used to do

We need a Code blue:
911 on the serious tip
for the scoundrels on the loose
the drive-by cowards
shooting at anyone…

Something real men just don't do!

September 16, 2001

We're looking for a
New normal
A new way to have hope
In the darkness
Whether in our beds
Or commuting on the
Train—passengers of a
Ride of faith draped
In fear and loathing

A new normal—

Adrian: Manchild in an Unpromised Land

Life was short and he played hard
Against all odds
Against all alarm
He played hard

He fought the good fight
And gave it his all
Against all odds
He played hard
The streets called
A force so strong
Even the good
can go wrong

He played hard
Life was short
Against all odds
Against all odds.

Cracks in the Crystal Stair

Not a gaping hole or a small snare/but a tension
pulled tight/snap stretched to tear: rip
it's there: cracks in the crystal stair

A glimpse
A wart
A pimple with
Pus

Rotting ooze
nasty drip
don't take a sip/rip
cracks in the crystal stair

Oh my, Gawd. My ancestors wail/moan/groan/and tremble
pain of us gone mad/sad/fumbling/tumbling
like old folks who have lost their way

Ouch! Oooh/weee/cracks in the crystal stair
my hair
gone bald and feeling disgraced
looks of hatred on my face... misery done to others
down on their luck/no time to bob, weave or duck

Kick and kiss
Kick and kiss
bring all the women down down down to their knees
"You know the position."
We know
You know
We know
the position of pain and foreboding
of life gone insane in the membrane
when cracks become windows
and windows become
flights to flee
the insanity of my being
of my paranoia
of women emasculating women
and thinking
"It's all good."

Cracks in the crystal stair
at least
I can get some
fresh air.

Moving Backwards to Forwards

The old people sit and stare
at a world gone mad:
people without homes
no place to be private
with themselves

Children selling drugs
and bringing the money home—
the baby needs milk
the family needs food
the world has gone mad

Decadence permeates the living room
television is in remote control
No limits to the language
and children learn
as they swagger to a gangster beat

The old people sit and stare
at progress since the back of the bus
No need to call—
"There's a colored person on channel 2…"
the world has gone mad

Painful Confessions

I ain't got no home
I am so lonely

I haven't got a bed
I am so tired
I can't wash myself;
I stink.

I can't brush my last teeth;
they rot

I can't bring a friend to dinner;
she's dead.

I can't change my panties;
I got only one pair.

I can't throw these old shoes away...
ain't no more.

I can't keep my baby...
no blanket

I can't live:
AIDS.

Eye Witness
(for our children)

I saw the innocence of the children
stolen in living color
a prime time crime

Their overalls backwards
their values twisted
all to a syncopated beat

I watched their souls kidnapped
I didn't dial 911…
I turned up the volume

Could this really be:
Unzipped pants; hands grabbing crotches
and the d.j. jammin' to give us more?

The boys turned into men
stunted in their spiritual growth…
but the beat goes on…

Stealing the innocence of children
in living color
in the prime of their time

E.J. Hobson

Lost Gold

She walks in the room
Her heart filled with gloom
Flyboy is dead
A satin pillow under his head

The faces are all of stone
His young widow sighs a moan
Flyboy is dead
A .38 split his head

The blood poured out like rain
His scream thundered out the pain
"Flyboy is dead,"
She whispered and bowed her head

He was our everything
The star who grasped the golden ring
Flyboy is dead
Miracles locked inside his head

The woman who shot him is free
She sits there across from me
Her eyes are dark and cold
She kept him from getting the gold

Justifiable homicide the court said
She didn't mean to shatter his head
But Flyboy is still dead
A community's heart is filled with dread

When they lowered him into the ground
No one made a single sound
Never again would he be around

To run a race like a gazelle
Faster than anyone could tell
He worked hard and long
But now Flyboy is long gone…

A Word to the Hip Hop Revolution

As we hip hop into a new century:

Will rappers be our griots
        filled with stories that bring
blessed magic to children

        huddled at their feet
        heaving on every word
        needing spirit weapons for war

It makes you think sometimes…

        Who will guide the children
        down mean streets strewn with
        technology, lasers, fiber optics
        mathematical calculations configured
        beyond our wildest imaginations

computers operating like right hands

Sometimes we need to know—

        that the truth will set us free
        that good guys do win in the end

that a stitch in time does save nine
that silver linings live in the cloud

that mama didn't lie:

there are days like this

Then maybe we will realize:

no lessons can go untaught
no child can just grow like a weed in the wind
the old Africans were right:
"it takes a whole village to raise a child"
isolationism will only kill us
the culture must be close to grow

As we hip hop into the twenty-first century:

there is a method to the madness
the fire next time is now
the problem of the color line draws
itself into the next millennium
we still keep hope alive
firing the pot for the end of the rainbow.

Tell Me

Tell me—
who said death was sweet
as it creeps
in the night

who said death was peaceful
when bullet racked bodies
swiggle in blood puddles
to speed up the life-leaving process

who said death
was anything
other than pain
lingering in the base
of the throat
long after the funeral crowd
has carried away
every edible item

Death is riotous
it stinks
it is ugly
when it stalks
your brother
in his 24th year

Epilogue

"Things fall apart; the center cannot hold."

—William Butler Yeats, The Second Coming

At Last. Self Portrait.

At last. Self portrait:
me alive and well
witnessing the zenith of
crossing boundaries
crashing through margins
leaving a blur around
edges rippled, ripped
and roaring.

At last. Self portrait:
me finally crossing
the threshold of my Jubilee.

All praises to community
helping hands outstretched
a human bridge of
human be-ing in the
moment with me.

At last. Self portrait:
sharp, clear,
in focus—a perfect 10
of connections and creativity
massaging margins,
blessing back the boundaries
and traveling through thresholds
of appreciation.
At last. Self portrait. Self aware!

The Golden Circle of the Soul Quake Experience

"I will even make a way in the wilderness, and rivers in the desert." Isaiah 43:19
It is with gratitude and thanks-giving for the Golden Circle.
You formed a human bridge across the chasm of vision and reality.

Kimberley Shareese Adams
Nas Inshirah Afi
Eleanor Andrews
Gilbert Balderramma
Frances A. Beard
Jo A. Berry-Segna
Linda & Lou Boitano
Clarence & Margarette Bolden
James H. Browdy
Patty Brown-Barnes
Rosalind A.Bryant
Michael Butera
Nesa Chappelle-Coombs
Russell & Lillian Clemons
Willie & Vivian Conner
Frances Dick
Warlene Gary
Rick Geier
Jim Geiger
Vince Giordano
Rich Gray
Dan Hand
Thomas R. Hardy II
Zernail & Cheryl Hardy
Jackie Harris
Deniese Hayes
Betty M. Jeung
Derrick Johnson
Betty & Lanny Lambdin
Antoinette Lee
Jim Loper

Kathleen Lyons
Evon Mazyck
Cheryl McLeod, Esq.
Marsha M. Meekins
Janet Morrison-Innis
Robert R. & Maria L. Muñoz
Carol Nelson
Debra Nixon
Beblon G. Parks
Rosa Sally Pickett
Becky Pringle
Cheryl Quick
Marlene Reagin, Ph.D.
David E. Reagin, M.D.
Judy K. Read
Harriet Sanford
Michael & Adriene Sears
Sheila Simmons, Ph.D.
Dino Smiley
Malcolm & Melita Staples
Curtis Symonds
Odessa Taylor
Lennell M. Terrell
Katrina Thompson
Theresa Turner
Marty Waltzer
Christopher Williams, Ph.D.
Pam Wilson
Chris Woods
Patricia A. Wright, Ed.D.
The Drew League

Closure

(for Branita Griffin Henson)

I write now
with the wings of the eagle

soaring

to new heights.

My spirit is free:

unbridled and real.

I am not afraid
to tap the water table
to take time
to breathe the colors
in my space
and on the turquoise horizon.

The air has cleared.
I feel the breeze blowing,
word magic in a new morning

filled with the promise of a future.